PRAYERS for YOU

THOMAS NELSON
Since 1798

INTRODUCTION

"I'm praying for you . . ."

"Please pray for me . . ."

We'll often say these words because we sincerely mean them, but other times we'll offer them because we're at a loss for words. What else can we say through life's most difficult circumstances? Sometimes there are no quick fixes, no pat answers or kind gestures. And so we offer prayer in hopes that it *might* help.

Might it help? Will it help?

The Bible tells us that prayer is never the wrong choice. Jesus prayed to His Father often, including in the hours leading up to His suffering and death on the cross (Matthew 26:39). God wants us to pray and intercede on behalf of one another, and He commands us to pray, with thanksgiving (Philippians 4:6–7), for healing (James 5:16), and for protection from temptation (Matthew 26:41). The Word tells us to pray on *every* occasion (Ephesians 6:18).

Prayer is *always* the right choice.

Prayers for You is a beautiful celebration of the fact that God wants you to talk to Him every day, all the time. Some of the prayers ask God for His help in times of pain and confusion, some praise Him for His wonderful ways, and others ask Him to help you cherish your dependency on Him for each day. Woven throughout are scriptures and quotes that give you comfort and peace no matter what you're facing. So find a quiet place and know that when you pray to God, He's hanging on your every word.

Never doubt what one prayer can do.

Start
each day
with a
grateful
heart.

You share
Your goodness with
those who make You
their sanctuary.

—Psalm 31:19 THE VOICE

Thank You, Lord,

for the life You've given us.

As I practice lifting my face to

You in joyful gladness each day,

I glimpse a little more freshly

that life here on Your beautiful

earth holds no value without

You as my Creator.

Time spent in prayer is never wasted.

—François Fénelon

Grant me, O Lord my God,
a mind to know you, a heart
to seek you, wisdom to find
you, conduct pleasing to you,
faithful perseverance in waiting
for you, and a hope of finally
embracing you. Amen.

—Thomas Aquinas

*My times
are in
Your hands,
O Lord.
I praise You.*

Let the words of my mouth and the meditation of my heart be acceptable in your sight, O Lord, my rock and my redeemer.

—Psalm 19:14 ESV

The LORD will fight for you; you need only to be still.

—Exodus 14:14 NIV

Lord, help me to cherish
these precious days of total
dependency on You. It is easy
to forget that they are a gift,
that You are, day by day,
teaching me to awaken every
morning with this request
on my heart: that You would
grant me Your perfect portion
for whatever the day holds.

Wonderful Counselor, Mighty God, Everlasting Father, Prince of Peace.

—Isaiah 9:6 NIV

No one can believe
how powerful prayer
is and what it can
effect, except those
who have learned
it by experience.
Whenever I have
prayed earnestly, I
have been heard and
have obtained more
than I prayed for. God
sometimes delays, but
he always comes.

—Martin Luther

Dear Lord, thank You for the gentle reminder that this life is temporary—and so are difficult circumstances. It is easy to feel overwhelmed because this life is all I know. Help me lift my eyes to You, from where my help comes.

—Inspired by Psalm 121:1

"I am leaving you with a gift—peace of mind and heart. And the peace I give is a gift the world cannot give. So don't be troubled or afraid."

—John 14:27 NLT

Don't trust
to hold God's hand;
Let Him do the holding . . .
and you the trusting.

—Hammer William
Webb-Peploe

Heavenly Father, I know
Your Word promises
that You will never
leave me, never forsake
me, but right now I
am feeling alone and
forgotten. Please renew
me. Refresh me. Help me
to sense Your presence
once again. Help me
to rejoice in You and
rest in Your grace.

"My grace
is sufficient
for you."

—2 Corinthians 12:9 NKJV

God will answer your prayers better than you think. Of course, one will not always get exactly what he has asked for. . . . We all have sorrows and disappointments, but one must never forget that, if commended to God, they will issue in good. . . . His own solution is far better than any we could conceive.

—Fanny J. Crosby

Lord, thank You for the privilege of a personal relationship with You. Help me not to take for granted the awe-inspiring right I have as Your child: to run to You, to be held tight, to be cradled lovingly in Your arms.

Prayer is an acknowledgment that our need of God's help is not partial but total.

—Alistair Begg

Hold on to Hope.

—Inspired by Romans 12:12

Lord, I'm struggling to remember that everything I experience is a gift from You, intended to do me good, not harm. It doesn't feel that way right now, but I long to be restored to that place of comfort and trust, where I know You have me exactly where You want me. I give myself to You now as my center, my focus, my true north. Thank You for never changing.

The Lord is my shepherd; there is nothing I lack.

—from Psalm 23:1 NABRE

Thy way, not mine,
O Lord, however dark
it be; lead me by thine
own hand; choose out
the path for me.

—Horatius Bonar

*Father, Your Word says
that times of tribulation
are opportunities to grow
in Christ. Help me to
learn and grow through
this time, remembering that
"the testing of [my] faith
produces endurance. And let
endurance have its perfect
result, so that [I] may be
perfect and complete,
lacking in nothing."*

—James 1:3–4 NASB

The Lord is my rock and my fortress and my deliverer; the God of my strength, in whom I will trust.

—2 Samuel 22:2–3 NKJV

Each time, before you intercede, be quiet first, and worship God in His glory. Think of what He can do, and how He delights to hear the prayers of His redeemed people. Think of your place and privilege in Christ, and expect great things!

—Andrew Murray

Lord, right now
I feel so overwhelmed.
Help me to rest in You.
Help me to remember that
You love me, that You are
with me even in my deepest
heartaches. Help me to
remember Your promise
that nothing "will be able
to separate [me] from the
love of God, which is in
Christ Jesus our Lord."

—Romans 8:39 NASB

The Lord gives
perfect peace
to those whose
faith is firm.

—Isaiah 26:3 CEV

The best and
sweetest flowers
of paradise God
gives to his people
when they are upon
their knees. Prayer is
the gate of heaven.

—Thomas Brooks

Father, I am so glad that You encourage—nay, command—me to cast my burdens on You. Your shoulders are broad and strong, and far more capable of carrying what troubles me. Thank You for instructing me in Your Word to lay my burdens at Your feet, and to exchange them for Your yoke, which is light and easy.

I find rest
in God;
only he
gives me hope.

—Psalm 62:5 NCV

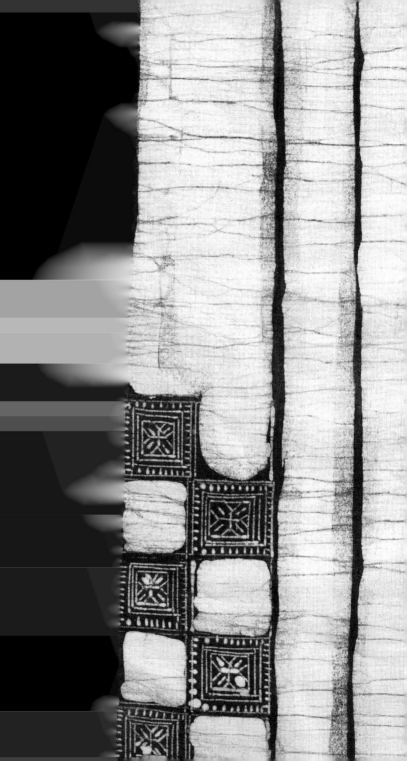

To reach the port of heaven, we must sail sometimes with the wind and sometimes against it—but we must sail, and not drift, nor lie at anchor.

—Oliver Wendell Holmes

*Lord Jesus,
may I cling
to nothing
but to You.*

No eye has seen,

nor ear heard,

nor the heart of

man imagined,

what God has

prepared for those

who love him.

—1 Corinthians 2:9 ESV

Peace does not mean to be in a place where there is no noise, trouble, or hard work. It means to be in the midst of all those things and still be calm in your heart.

—Unknown

Lord, I am confused
by the circumstances
of my life right now.
Please give me Your
wisdom. As I walk
through this trial,
please teach me what
You want me to learn.
Help me to lean on You
every step of the way.

The joy of the

LORD is your

strength.

—Nehemiah 8:10 NASB

We know not
what prayer
can do.

—Charles Spurgeon

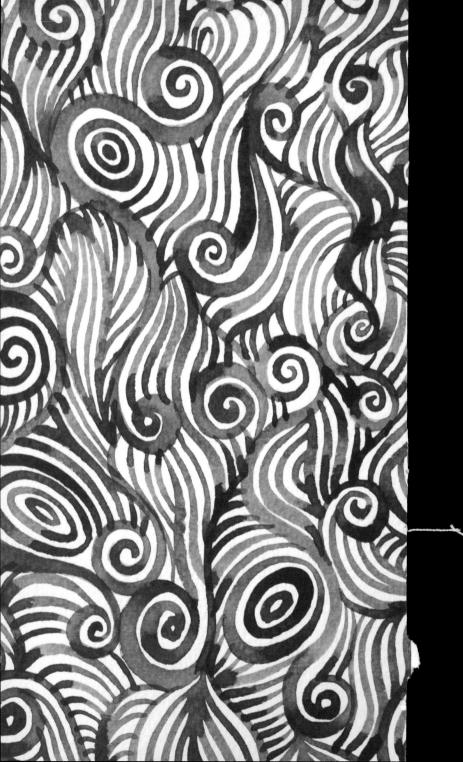

Lord, keep my heart with You.

"I will not cause
pain without
allowing something
new to be born,"
says the Lord.

—Isaiah 66:9 NCV

Do what you can
and pray
for what you
cannot yet do.

—Augustine

Lord, You are my stronghold. I envision myself clinging to You during this season of pain and uncertainty. You are my rock, my refuge. When everything around me seems to be falling apart, I know that You have me right where You want me . . . and I trust You.

Hope
anchors
the soul.

—Inspired by
Hebrews 6:19 NASB

To persist in prayer
without returns,
this is not time lost,
but a great gain.
It is endeavor without
thought of self and
only for the glory
of the Lord.

—St. Teresa of Avila

Live each

day with

gratitude.

You have
redeemed me,
O Lord God
of truth.

—Psalm 31:5 NKJV

Desire only the
will of God;
seek him alone
and supremely,
and you will
find peace.

—François Fenelon

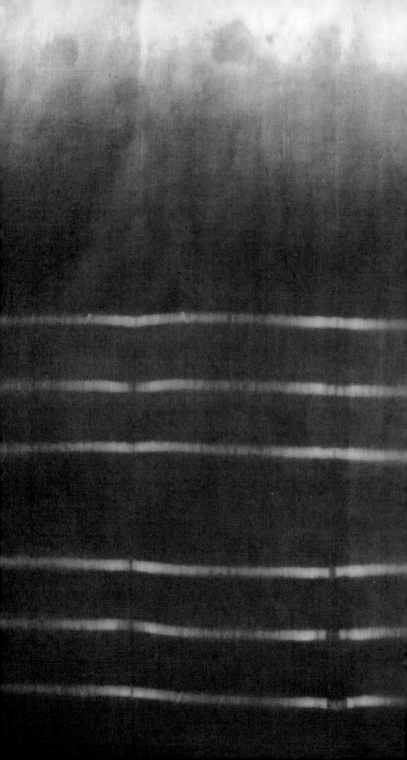

Lord, I need You. My desire is to glorify You, but I am incapable of doing that through my own effort. Please bear me up and give me Your strength. Lift my head and help me to rejoice in You.

The steadfast love of the LORD never ceases; his mercies never come to an end; they are new every morning.

—Lamentations 3:22–23 ESV

Prayer should be the means by which I, at all times, receive all that I need, and, for this reason, be my daily refuge, my daily consolation, my daily joy, my source of rich and inexhaustible joy in life.

—John Chrysostom

Lord, I find comfort
in knowing that
You alone can give
me peace that surpasses
my understanding.
I rest in that knowledge,
take solace in it,
and trust You for it.

"Have I not commanded you? Be strong and courageous. Do not be frightened, and do not be dismayed, for the Lord your God is with you wherever you go."

—Joshua 1:9 ESV

Lord, make me
an instrument
of thy peace.

—Francis of Assisi

I love You, Jesus.

Help me to love

You more and

more, to trust You

more and more,

and to listen

ever more keenly

to Your voice.

Be strong and courageous. Do not fear. . .for it is the Lord your God who goes with you. He will not leave you or forsake you.

—Deuteronomy 31:6 ESV

O Lord, my God, my
only hope, hear me,
lest through weariness I
should not wish to seek
you. . . . Give me the
strength to seek, you
who have caused me to
find you, and have given
me the hope of finding
you more and more.

—Augustine

Thank You, Father, for friends who uplift, encourage, support, and pray for me when I don't know how to pray. They are an embodiment of Romans 12:12—"Rejoice in hope, be patient in tribulation, be constant in prayer" (ESV). Please shape me into this kind of prayer warrior for others.

"When you pass through the waters, I will be with you; and through the rivers, they shall not overflow you. When you walk through the fire, you shall not be burned, nor shall the flame scorch you."

—Isaiah 43:2 NKJV

Faith in a prayer-hearing God will make a prayer-loving Christian.

—Andrew Murray

Open your
heart to hope.

Your ways, O Lord,
make known to me.
Teach me Your paths.
Guide me in Your
truth and teach me,
for You are God my
Savior, and for You
I wait all the day.

—Inspired by Psalm 25:4–5

You need not
cry very loud;
He is nearer to us
than we think.

—Brother Lawrence

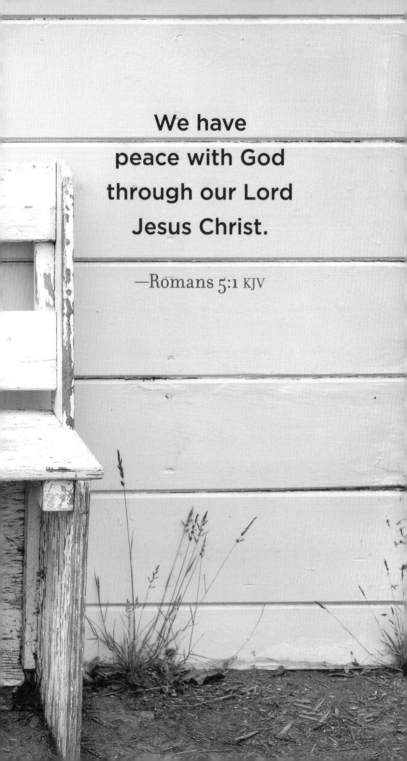

We have
peace with God
through our Lord
Jesus Christ.

—Romans 5:1 KJV

In all things
it is better
to hope
than despair.

—Johann Wolfgang
von Goethe

Christ in you,
the hope of glory.

—Colossians 1:27 NKJV

When I cannot read,
when I cannot think,
when I cannot even
pray, I can trust.

—J. Hudson Taylor

"Be always on the watch, and pray."

—Luke 21:36 NIV

The prayer that
begins with trustfulness,
and passes on into
waiting, will always
end in thankfulness,
triumph, and praise.

—Alexander MacLaren

If God is for us,
who can
be against us?

—Romans 8:31 NKJV

Four things let us ever keep in mind: God hears prayer, God heeds prayer, God answers prayer, and God delivers by prayer.

—E. M. Bounds

He gives power to
the weak, and to
those who have no
might He increases
strength.

—Isaiah 40:29 NKJV

The greatest answer to prayer is that I am brought into a perfect understanding with God, and that alters my view of actual things.

—Oswald Chambers

The LORD
has heard my
cry for mercy;
the LORD accepts
my prayer.

—Psalm 6:9 NIV

Prayer is the
breath of the
new creature.

—Richard Baxter

For the Eternal is always there to protect you. He will safeguard your each and every step.

—Proverbs 3:26

THE VOICE

Pray the largest prayers. You cannot think a prayer so large that God, in answering it, will not wish you had made it larger. Pray not for crutches but for wings.

—Phillips Brooks

The Lord
stood with
me and gave
me strength.

—2 Timothy 4:17 NLT

Prayer is beyond any
question the highest
activity of the human
soul. Man is at his greatest
and highest when upon
his knees he comes
face to face with God.

—D. Martyn Lloyd-Jones

"Be still,
and know
that
I am God."

—Psalm 46:10 NKJV

It is not only our duty to
pray for others, but also
to desire the prayers of
others for ourselves.

—William Gurnall

Do not be afraid
of tomorrow, for God
is already there.

To fall in love with God is the greatest of all romances; to seek him, the greatest adventure; to find him, the greatest human achievement.

—Augustine

Like burning incense, Lord, let my prayer rise up to You.

—Inspired by Psalm 141:2

O Lord my God,
teach my heart
this day where and
how to see You, where
and how to find You.

—St. Anselm

Prayer is the natural and joyous
breathing of the spiritual
life by which the heavenly
atmosphere is inhaled and
then exhaled in prayer.

—Andrew Murray

Every day I will bless You, and I will praise Your name forever and ever.

—Psalm 145:2 NASB